100+

TIPS · IDEAS

BATHROOMS

BAÑOS

SALLES DE BAINS

BADEZIMMER

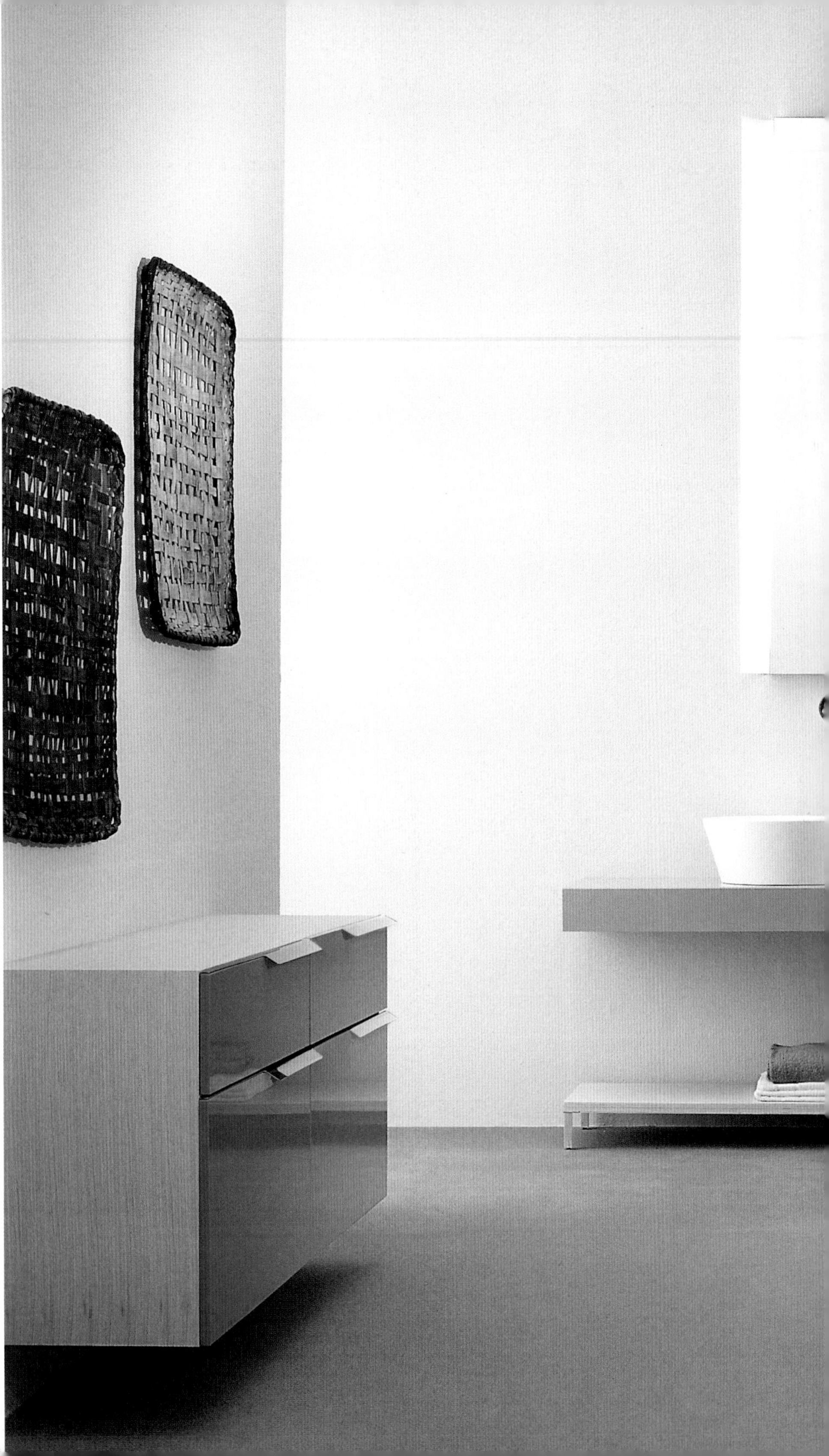

AUTHORS
Fernando de Haro & Omar Fuentes

EDITORIAL DESIGN & PRODUCTION
AM Editores S.A. de C.V.

PROJECT MANAGERS
Valeria Degregorio Vega
Tzacil Cervantes Ortega

COORDINATION
Edali Nuñez Daniel
Martha Guerrero Martel

COPYWRITERS
Abraham Orozco
Roxana Villalobos

ENGLISH TRANSLATION
Louis Loizides

FRENCH TRANSLATION
Wordgate Translations

GERMAN TRANSLATION
Heike Ruttkowski

EDITORES

PUBLISHERS

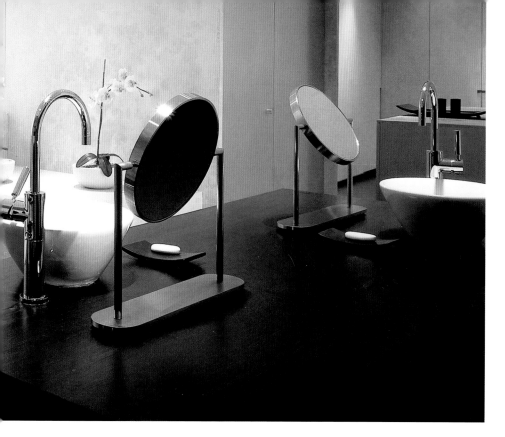

100+ TIPS · IDEAS
bathrooms . baños
salles de bains . badezimmer

© 2009, Fernando de Haro & Omar Fuentes
AM Editores S.A. de C.V.
Paseo de Tamarindos 400 B, suite 102, Col. Bosques de las Lomas, C.P. 05120, México, D.F.
Tels. 52(55) 5258 0279, Fax. 52(55) 5258 0556. ame@ameditores.com **www.ameditores.com**

ISBN 13: 978-607-437-020-1

Printed in China.

INTRODUCTION
INTRODUCCIÓN
INTRODUCTION
EINLEITUNG

It was not until the Nineteenth Century that hygiene started being regarded as a priority and bathrooms given their own specific place in homes, and, even so, they were still considered independent from the rest of the house. Following centuries of gradual progress, bathrooms today are designed to satisfy the needs of the most demanding users and have become a private haven in which peacefulness and harmony reign. Bathrooms offer a range of options in terms of look and style, including classical, avant-garde, rustic to take you back to the past, or highly innovative, which looks more towards the future. Any good option will make the most of technological breakthroughs centered on this part of the house, as well as the use of materials and coatings that are waterproof and damp proof and play a significant esthetic role.

The bathroom is no longer a place that needs to be concealed. It is now a space that proudly parades its decorative prowess and responds to the preferences and personality of its users. They comprise spacious and well-defined areas, often small rooms with highly practical, versatile and mobile solutions that can be adapted to the size of industrial lofts that are currently very much in vogue. Bathrooms ultimately perform their role adequately, but without overlooking their status as places of rest and relaxation.

La higiene no fue considerada una prioridad sino hasta entrado el siglo XIX, cuando los baños empezaron a ocupar un sitio propio, aunque todavía considerado como un espacio independiente del resto de la casa. Luego de una lenta evolución, el baño de nuestros días se adapta a las máximas exigencias de los usuarios y se ha transformado en un paraíso privado donde reina la paz. Existen múltiples propuestas que permiten disponer de un baño con reminiscencias clásicas o uno muy vanguardista, de estilo rústico con una mirada al pasado o muy innovadores con una tendencia futurista, pero siempre aprovechando los avances tecnológicos en las instalaciones sanitarias y el uso de materiales y revestimientos de gran valor estético y resistentes a la humedad y al agua. El baño ha dejado de ser una habitación oculta para convertirse en un espacio que se equipa con una intención decorativa y que responde al gusto y la personalidad de los usuarios; amplias habitaciones con zonas bien delimitadas, pequeños cuartos con soluciones muy prácticas o propuestas móviles y versátiles adaptables a las dimensiones de los lofts de tipo industrial de moda hoy en día. Baños, al fin y al cabo, que desempeñan adecuadamente su función sin dejar de ser zonas de relajamiento y descanso.

L'hygiène n'a jamais été considérée comme une priorité en soi avant les premières décennies du XIXème siècle lorsque l'on a commencé prendre en compte l'espace occupé par la salle de bain, pièce que l'on considérait cependant comme un endroit indépendant du reste de la maison. Après avoir lentement évolué, la salle de bain, de nos jours, répond aux demandes les plus spécifiques des usagers et s'est transformée en un lieu privé et paradisiaque ou règne la tranquillité. Les styles architecturaux et décoratifs d'une salle de bain peuvent être multiples : classique, avant-gardiste, rustique et rappelant le passé ou très innovateur avec une certaine tendance futuriste. Mais dans tous les cas, on sait profiter des avancées technologiques en ce qui concerne les installations sanitaires et l'utilisation de matériaux et de revêtements esthétiques et résistants à l'humidité et à l'eau. Aujourd'hui, la salle de bain n'est plus la pièce que l'on dissimulait mais un endroit dont la décoration a été pensée pour répondre aux attentes et à la personnalité de ses hôtes. Elle peut prendre l'apparence d'une grande pièce divisée en espaces bien délimités, d'un lieu de petite taille très pratique ou d'un emplacement modulable et multifonctionnel qui peut s'adapter à l'usage très à la mode actuellement que l'on fait des anciens lofts industriels de grande taille. Pour finir, la salle de bain est aussi aujourd'hui un lieu à la fois très fonctionnel et un endroit de détente et de repos.

Die Hygiene wurde erst ab dem XIX. Jahrhundert als Priorität betrachtet, als ein eigens dazu eingerichteter Ort als Badezimmer genutzt wurde, obwohl es sich immernoch um einen Bereich gehandelt hat, der vom Rest des Hauses unabhängig war. Nach Durchlaufen einer langsamen Evolution, befriedigt das Badezimmer unserer heutigen Zeit auch die ausgefallensten Bedürfnisse der Benutzer und hat sich in ein privates Paradies verwandelt, in dem Frieden herrscht. In Bezug auf die Einrichtung eines Badezimmers sind vielfältige Möglichkeiten vorhanden, wobei ein klassischer oder sehr avantgardistischer Touch zum Einsatz kommen kann. Ferner kann das Bad rustikal mit einem Blick auf die Vergangenheit eingerichtet werden oder sehr modern mit einer Ausrichtung in die Zukunft. Dabei wird aber stets der technische Fortschritt im Bereich der sanitären Anlagen genutzt, sowie Materialien und Verkleidungen mit grossem ästhetischem Wert, die gleichzeitig resistent gegen Wasser und Feuchtigkeit sind. Das Badezimmer ist kein versteckter Raum mehr, sondern vielmehr ein Bereich, der mit einer dekorativen Absicht ausgestattet wird und der dem Geschmack und der Persönlichkeit der Benutzer entspricht. Dabei sind geräumige Zimmer denkbar, die gut abgegrenzte Bereiche aufweisen oder kleine Räume mit sehr praktischen Lösungen; oder bewegliche und wandelbare Einrichtungen, die sich an die Ausmasse der Loftwohnungen vom industriellen Typ anpassen, die heutzutage modern sind. Dabei geht es um Badezimmer, die letztendlich ihre Funktion auf geeignete Weise erfüllen, ohne die Entspannung und Erholung zu vernachlässigen.

The colors used in a bathroom can have a profound effect on the impression it generates. Lighter tones will create a feeling of spaciousness, while darker ones will make the bathroom seem smaller than it actually is. Soft colors are relaxing and create a bright and lively ambience. Stronger colors are revitalizing and provide an atmosphere characterized by elegance and personality.

Classic options tend to favor soft tones, such as blue and bright green, or neutral tones that evoke the sea and sand. Other possibilities focus on more formal colors, such as black and gray, to create a stylish and distinguished setting. Yellow tones, along with whites and a range of raw colors, will have a luminous effect. There are also some very innovative trends, with no walls and open spaces, that prefer stronger colors like red or more daring color combinations.

La elección de los colores en un baño puede alterar ostensiblemente la percepción de quines la ocupan; los tonos claros transmiten la sensación de amplitud y los oscuros parecen empequeñecerlo; los colores suaves relajan el ánimo y crean un ambiente luminoso y vivaz; los colores más fuertes reaniman y proporcionan un ambiente elegante y con personalidad.

Las opciones más clásicas se inclinan por los tonos suaves como el azul, el verde claro o los tonos neutros que remiten al agua del mar y la arena. Otras propuestas se inclinan por colores más formales como el negro o los grises, que crean un ambiente elegante y distinguido. Los amarillos, igual que la gama de blancos y crudos provocan espacios luminosos. Y aun existen las tendencias muy innovadoras, con espacios abiertos y sin paredes que se inclinan por los tonos fuertes, como el rojo, o por audaces combinaciones multicolores.

Le choix de la couleur peut énormément changer notre façon de voir une salle de bain. Les teintes claires paraissent agrandir la pièce alors que les couleurs foncées au contraire la réduisent. Les tons pastel font de la pièce un endroit calme, lumineux et vivant alors que les couleurs plus vives transforment la salle de bain en un lieu plein d'énergie avec une élégance personnalisée.

Opter pour une couleur claire comme le bleu, le vert ou des tons neutres qui rappellent l'eau de mer ou le sable fin est une décision tout ce qu'il y a de plus classique. On peut aussi choisir des couleurs plus austères comme le noir et certains gris pour faire de la salle de bain une pièce élégante et raffinée. Les jaunes, à l'instar de certains blancs ou autres couleurs pâles, illuminent l'espace. Notre choix peut aussi refléter les dernières tendances en matière de décoration avec des pièces ouvertes et sans séparations et des couleurs vives comme le rouge ou, pourquoi pas, des mélanges polychromes audacieux.

Die Wahl der Farben im Badezimmer kann die Wahrnehmung der Benutzer wesentlich beeinflussen. Helle Farben vermitteln den Eindruck von Weite und dunkle Farben machen den Raum optisch kleiner. Weiche Farbtöne wirken entspannend und führen zu einer strahlenden und lebendigen Atmosphäre. Stärkere Farbtöne beleben und sorgen für eine eleganten Atmosphäre mit Persönlichkeit.

Die klassischeren Möglichkeiten neigen zu weichen Farben, wie blau, hellgrün und neutralen Farben, die an Meerwasser und Sand erinnern. Andere Vorschläge machen Gebrauch von formelleren Farben, wie schwarz oder grau, die zu einer eleganten und edlen Atmosphäre führen. Gelb sowie Weiss- und Naturtöne verleihen dem Raum einen strahlenden Touch. Und dann sind da noch die ganz modernen Tendenzen mit offenen Bereichen ohne Wände, bei denen starke Farben zur Andwendung kommen, wie rot oder ganz gewagte, bunte Kombinationen.

Light tones combine with polished surfaces to bring out the light and space of the bathroom to the full.

Los tonos claros y las superficies pulidas logran que el baño sea más luminoso y dé la sensación de amplitud.

Les teintes claires et les surfaces polies parviennent à illuminer et à agrandir la salle de bain.

Helle Farbtöne und polierte Oberflächen führen dazu, dass das Badezimmer heller wirkt und den Eindruck von Geräumigkeit vermittelt.

TIPS · ASTUCES · TIPPS
- *White is the color that provides the broadest spectrum of benefits and sensations for the bathroom.*
- *El color blanco es el que mayores ventajas y sensaciones ofrece a un baño.*
- *Le blanc est la couleur la plus indiquée pour une salle de bain parce qu'elle en souligne les qualités et les atmosphères qui lui sont associées.*
- *Die weisse Farbe bietet im Bereich des Badezimmers die meisten Vorteile, sowie auch die vorteilhaftesten Eindrücke.*

Darkly colored
wooden furnishings
and walls provide
a pleasant contrast
with the white of
the furniture and
accessories to
generate a stylish
and distinguished
ambience.

Los colores oscuros
en el mobiliario
de madera y en
los muros, ofrecen
un agradable
contraste con el
blanco de las
tarjas, tinas e
inodoros para
crear un ambiente
distinguido y
elegante.

Les meubles en
bois et les murs,
tout deux de
couleur foncée,
contrastent
agréablement
avec le blanc des
accessoires de la
salle de bain pour
faire de la pièce
un lieu raffiné et
élégant.

Dunkle Farbtöne
an Möbeln und
Wänden führen zu
einem angenehmen
Kontrast mit den
weissen Einrichtungs-
gegenständen
und Accessoires.
Insgesamt entsteht eine
elegante und edle
Atmosphäre.

TIPS - ASTUCES - TIPPS
• *Reddish tones on the walls will highlight the faucets.*
• *Recuerda que los tonos rojizos en muros hacen que la grifería resalte.*
• *Un rappel: les tons rouges sur un mur mettent en valeur la robinetterie.*
• *Rote Farbtöne an den Wänden lassen die Armaturen besonders zur Geltung kommen.*

The Zen look is centered on a minimal number of carefully selected items.

La estética zen se expresa con un mínimo de elementos cuidadosamente seleccionados.

Le style « zen », c'est un nombre minimum d'éléments choisis avec soin.

Die Zen-Ästhetik basiert auf einem Mindestmass an auserwählten Elementen.

TIPS - ASTUCES - TIPPS
- *Even though the way it is installed is no secret, a floating basin will always boast a magical feel.*
- *Aunque se conozca su forma de instalación, un lavabo flotante siempre luce mágico.*
- *La pose d'un lavabo suspendu n'a rien de mystérieux mais l'effet produit reste toujours magique.*
- *Obwohl man weiss, wie es installiert wurde, sieht ein schwebendes Waschbecker immer magisch aus.*

Rough textures and colors afford this bathroom a more traditional feel.

Los colores y las texturas rugosas confieren a este baño un aire tradicional.

Les murs et les textures non polis donnent à cette salle de bain un aspect traditionnel.

Rauhe Farben und Texturen verleihen diesem Badezimmer einen traditionellen Touch.

TIPS - ASTUCES - TIPPS

- The tone and textures of natural fibers are a superb option for bathrooms.
- El tono y las texturas de las fibras naturales son muy adecuados para baños.
- Les tons et la texture des fibres naturelles sont particulièrement recommandés pour les salles de bain.
- Der Farbton und die Texturen der Naturfasern sind ausgesprochen geeignet für Bäder.

The large window and the mirrors visually enhance the space, while dark tones add a touch of warmth.

La gran ventana y los espejos amplían visualmente el espacio y los tonos oscuros proporcionan calidez al ambiente.

La grande fenêtre et les miroirs semblent agrandir la pièce et les teintes foncées lui donnent un aspect plus confortable.

Das grosse Fenster und die Spiegel vergrössern visuell den Raum und die dunklen Farbtöne verleihen der Atmosphäre Wärme.

Different materials, such as wood, marble, glass and steel, blend perfectly to provide an original and elegant setting.

Los diferentes materiales, maderas, mármoles, cristal, acero, se complementan para crear un ambiente original.

Les différents matériaux comme les bois, les marbres, le verre et l'acier se complémentent pour faire de la pièce un lieu raffiné et original.

Die verschiedenen Materialien, wie Holz, Marmor, Glas und Stahl, ergänzen sich und schaffen eine edle und originelle Atmosphäre.

TIPS - ASTUCES - TIPPS
- *White and chocolate brown are extremes that look great when used together.*
- *Blanco y chocolate son extremos que juntos lucen atractivos.*
- *L'association entre les couleurs opposées que sont le blanc et le chocolat est très séduisante.*
- *Weiss und Braun sind Extreme, die zusammen attraktiv aussehen.*

FUNCTION

FUNCIÓN

FONCTION

FUNKTION

Bathrooms have been transformed in recent years as a result of cultural factors and customs, but also because of comfort and sheer pleasure. They are now designed to suit the tastes and preferences of users, and are projected in spacious, light-filled rooms with large windows, views of the garden and unique furniture. Inhabitants can enjoy the usual functional purposes of their bathroom, but now there are the added benefits of rest and relaxation, as well as furniture for storage, changing facilities, tubs for massages and room for socializing.

The bathroom has been designed for simultaneous use by different members of the family, but without sacrificing the intimacy required for personal activities. The design allows it to be divided into specific zones, such as the washbasin shelf, the tub or shower and the toilet areas. The first one is usually located near the door, as is requires less intimacy. The shower occupies a different area, as does the toilet, which is now made with highly decorative designs.

Los baños han sufrido una completa transformación en los últimos años, no sólo por cuestiones de cultura o costumbre sino también por razones de comodidad y placer. Hoy, los baños se diseñan de acuerdo con el gusto y las preferencias de los usuarios, se proyectan en amplias habitaciones llenas de luz, con grandes ventanales, vista al jardín y muebles exclusivos. Los moradores de una casa pueden dar al baño el uso funcional de siempre, pero al mismo tiempo convertirlo en una zona de relajamiento y descanso, con muebles de guardado, vestidor, tinas de masaje y espacio para la convivencia.

El diseño permite que el cuarto de baño pueda ser usado por diferentes miembros de la familia a la vez sin tener que renunciar a la intimidad que exige una estancia de servicio exclusivo. El diseño permite dividir cómodamente el espacio en zonas específicas como la de tocador, la de aguas, con bañera o ducha incluidas y la reservada para sanitarios. La primera se sitúa generalmente cerca de la puerta, puesto que requiere menos intimidad; otra más reservada para la ducha y finalmente, la del sanitario cuyo diseño es hoy, incluso, altamente decorativo.

Les salles de bain ont connu un profond changement ces dernières années qui s'explique par des mentalités et des habitudes nouvelles mais aussi par la recherche du fonctionnel et du confort. Aujourd'hui, les salles de bain sont pensées en accord avec les goûts de ceux qui les utilisent. Ce sont de grandes pièces bien éclairées, avec d'amples fenêtres qui donnent sur le jardin et avec des meubles particuliers. Les personnes qui résident dans un lieu peuvent choisir de faire de la salle de bain une pièce avant tout pratique comme auparavant mais ils peuvent aussi décider d'en faire un endroit pour la détente et le repos avec des meubles de rangement, un dressing, une baignoire balnéo et un coin salon. La conception de certaines salles de bain est pensée de telle façon qu'elle permet l'utilisation de cette pièce par plusieurs personnes de la même famille en même temps sans que personne ne renonce à son intimité, qualité primordiale pour un lieu de ce genre. On peut diviser l'endroit pour créer des espaces pratiques et spécifiques comme celui du cabinet de toilette, des lavabos, de la baignoire ou de la douche ou encore celui des sanitaires. Le cabinet de toilette se situe généralement près de la porte car l'intimité n'est pas ce que l'on y recherche contrairement à la douche et aux w.c., ces derniers étant d'ailleurs aujourd'hui conçus comme faisant complètement partie de la décoration.

Die Badezimmer haben in den letzten Jahren eine komplette Transformation durchgemacht, nicht nur aufgrund der Kultur und der Gewohnheiten, sondern auch aufgrund der Bequemlichkeit und des Genusses. Heutzutage werden die Badezimmer in Übereinstimmung mit dem Geschmack und den Vorlieben der Benutzer designed; sie werden in geräumigen Zimmern mit viel Licht geplant, mit grossen Fenstern, Blick auf den Garten und exklusiven Möbeln. Die Hausbewohner benutzen das Badezimmer für die gleichen Zwecke wie dies schon immer der Fall war, aber gleichzeitig handelt es sich dabei auch um einen Bereich der Entspannung und der Erholung, mit Möbeln zum Aufbewahren, Ankleidebereich, Massage-Badewanne und Platz für das Zusammensein. Das Design ermöglicht es, dass das Badezimmer von den verschiedenen Familienmitgliedern gleichzeitig genutzt werden kann, ohne dass dabei auf die Privatsphäre verzichtet werden muss. Durch das Design werden die Bereiche bequem in verschiedene Zonen aufgeteilt, mit Toilette, Waschbecken, Badewanne und Dusche zusammen und Toilette davon abgetrennt. Ersterer Bereich befindet sich für gewöhnlich in der Nähe der Tür, da hier weniger Privatsphäre nötig ist; die Dusche befindet sich etwas weiter abseits und schliesslich die Toilette, deren Design heutzutage äusserst dekorativ ist.

TIPS - ASTUCES - TIPPS
- *Raised bathroom furniture makes it easier to clean the lower areas.*
- *Los muebles de baño volados facilitan la limpieza de las áreas inferiores.*
- *Les meubles sans pied dans une salle de bain facilitent le nettoyage des sols.*
- *Hängende Badezimmermöbel erleichtern die Reinigung der unteren Bereiche.*

The same space
is shared by
the shower and
a comfortable
hydromassage
unit, both made in
the same style and
material.

La ducha comparte
el espacio con una
confortable tina
de hidromasaje
de idéntico estilo y
material.

L'espace est
partagé entre
une douche
très pratique et
une baignoire
hydromassage
de style identique
et fabriquées
avec les mêmes
matériaux.

Die Dusche
teilt sich den
Bereich mit
einer bequemen
Hydromassage-
Badewanne, die
den gleichen Stil
und das gleiche
Material aufweist.

TIPS - ASTUCES - TIPPS
• Integrating the bathtub and the shower unit is both original and functional.
• Integrar la tina y la regadera en dos niveles es tan original como funcional.
• Placer la baignoire et la douche sur deux niveaux est aussi original que fonctionnel.
• Die Badewanne und die Dusche auf zwei Ebenen zu integrieren, ist genauso originell wie funktionell.

TIPS - ASTUCES - TIPPS
- The inclusion of two basins in the bathroom will allow you to share personal hygiene and getting ready to go out with your partner.
- Si incluyes dos lavabos tendrás la posibilidad de compartir con tu pareja el aseo y el arreglo.
- Opter pour deux lavabos, c'est la possibilité de pouvoir converser avec votre compagnon au moment de la toilette et des derniéres retouches avant de sortir.
- Wenn zwei Waschbecken vorgesehen werden, besteht die Möglichkeit, die Körperpflege zur gleichen Zeit wie der Partner vorzunehmen.

The furniture has been designed and arranged in a way that allows it to be used by more than one person at a time.

La disposición y el diseño del mobiliario hace posible que las instalaciones se usen por más de una persona a la vez.

La disposition et le design du mobilier permettent l'utilisation de l'endroit par plusieurs personnes en même temps.

Die Aufteilung und das Design der Möbel ermöglichen es, dass die Installationen durch mehr als eine Person gleichzeitig genutzt werden können.

TIPS - ASTUCES - TIPPS
- *Single faucets are discrete and work very well indeed.*
- *Ten en cuenta que los grifos monomando son discretos y funcionan muy bien.*
- *N'oubliez pas que les robinets mitigeurs sont à la fois discrets et très fonctionnels.*
- *Es ist in Betracht zu ziehen, dass Mischbatterien dezent sind und gut funktionieren.*

The spacious changing room is ideal for storing clothes and bathroom items.

Los amplios muebles del vestidor permiten almacenar cómodamente ropa y utensilios para el baño.

Les meubles de grande taille du dressing permettent un rangement commode des vêtements et des articles de toilette.

Die geräumigen Möbel des Ankleideraumes ermöglichen es, die Handtücher und Utensilien des Badezimmers bequem unterzubringen.

This bathroom has been designed to contain different intimate spaces in the same place.

El diseño permite la presencia de diferentes espacios íntimos en un solo lugar.

Le design de cette salle de bain permet que différents espaces intimes existent dans un même lieu.

Das Design ermöglicht das Vorhandensein verschiedener privater Bereiche an einem Ort.

TIPS - ASTUCES - TIPPS

• *Any wood used in the damp areas must be damp-proof.*
• *Si colocas madera en el área húmeda asegúrate que ésta sea resistente a la humedad.*
• *Si vous choisissez le bois pour une pièce humide, soyez sûrs qu'il y résistera bien.*
• *Wenn in der Feuchtzone Holz angebracht wird, ist darauf zu achten, dass dies widerstandsfähig gegen Feuchtigkeit ist.*

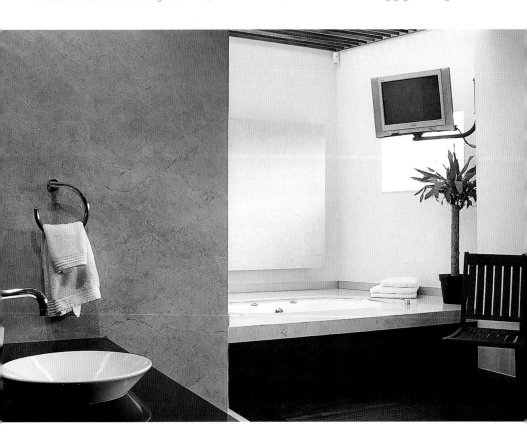

The fine wood and glass of the wardrobe next to the bathroom provide an excellent space arrangement option.

Las finas maderas y el cristal del armario anexo al cuarto de baño, en una inteligente ordenación del espacio.

Une façon intelligente d'organiser l'espace : des bois fins associés à du verre pour une armoire contigüe à la salle de bain.

Edles Holz und das Glas des Schrankes, der an das Badezimmer angrenzt, organisieren auf intelligente Art und Weise den Raum.

TIPS · ASTUCES · TIPPS
- *A modulated item of furniture for storage is a good way of keeping things in order.*
- *Recuerda que un mueble de guardar modulado obliga a mantener el orden.*
- *N'oubliez pas qu'un meuble de rangement modulable sous-entend une pièce toujours en ordre.*
- *Ein modulares Möbel zum Aufbewahren verpflichtet dazu Ordnung zu halten.*

This room performs a multiple role as a bathroom, changing room and storage facility for clothes and bathroom articles.

La habitación desempeña la múltiple función de cuarto de baño, vestidor y zona para guardar ropa y utensilios.

Une pièce multifonctionnelle qui sert à la fois de salle de bain, de dressing et d'endroit pour ranger les vêtements et les articles de toilette.

Der Raum hat die vielfältige Funktion gleichzeitig Badezimmer, Ankleidezimmer und Bereich zum Unterbringen von Handtüchern und Utensilien zu sein.

TIPS · ASTUCES · TIPPS
- Make the most of the space in a rectangular bathroom by putting mirrors on the longer walls.
- Dota de amplitud a un baño rectangular colocando espejos en los laterales más largos.
- Des miroirs sur les murs latéraux d'une salle de bain rectangulaire l'agrandissent.
- Ein rechteckiges Badezimmer sieht grösser aus, wenn an den längeren Seiten Spiegel angebracht werden.

This wooden item of furniture stands alone like an island to guard over the brightly-lit bathroom.

Un mueble de madera, en forma de isla, preside el luminoso espacio de este baño.

Un meuble en bois, telle une île, trône au centre de cette lumineuse salle de bain.

Der grosse Spiegel mit Rahmen aus dunklem Holz kombiniert mit dem Möbel zum Aufbewahren und vervielfacht das Licht, das durch das Fenster mit Blick in den Garten eindringt.

TIPS - ASTUCES - TIPPS
- A massage bed can be a very seductive as well as practical option for the bathroom.
- Muy seductora y práctica podrá resultar una cama de masajes en el baño.
- Un accessoire raffiné et pratique : une table de massage dans la salle de bain.
- Eine Massageliege im Badezimmer kann sehr verführerisch und praktisch sein.

The space is big enough to accommodate both common areas and zones set aside for personal usage, turning the bathroom into a multifunctional location.

Las dimensiones del espacio permiten disponer de áreas comunes y zonas reservadas para uso personal y convierten el baño en una habitación multifuncional.

Les dimensions généreuses de la pièce permettent le voisinage de pièces communes et privées pour un usage personnel et font de cet endroit un espace multifonctionnel.

Die Ausmasse des Raumes ermöglichen es, Gemeinschaftsbereiche und private Bereiche vorzusehen; so verwandelt sich das Badezimmer in einen multifunktionellen Raum.

TIPS · ASTUCES · TIPPS
- *If you install your washbasin on an isle, you need to make sure the space around it is unobstructed.*
- *Si colocas los lavabos en una isla, cerciórate que el espacio de circulación sea holgado.*
- *Si vous décidez de ne pas placer les lavabos contre le mur, assurez-vous qu'il y ait suffisamment de place pour circuler.*
- *Werden die Waschbecken auf einer Insel angebracht, so muss sichergegangen werden, dass der begehbare Bereich gross genug ist.*

Abundant
daylight from the
roof and large
windows makes
personal hygiene
a more enjoyable
affair.

La abundante
luz natural,
proveniente del
techo y grandes
ventanas, hace
más placentera
la aparentemente
simple función del
aseo personal.

Une importante
lumière naturelle qui
vient du plafond et
des grandes fenêtres
pour que le fait
apparemment simple
de veiller à son
hygiène personnelle
soit plus agréable.

Das reichliche
natürliche Licht stammt
von der Decke und den
grossen Fenstern und
macht die scheinbar
einfache Funktion
der persönlichen
Körperpflege
angenehmer.

TIPS - ASTUCES - TIPPS
- A towel rack is a vital element in the damp area of the bathroom, whatever its style may be.
- Un toallero, sea cual sea su estilo, es un elemento indispensable en zonas húmedas de baños.
- Un porte-serviettes, quel que soit son style, est un accessoire indispensable pour la salle de bain.
- Ein Handtuchständer -gleichgültig welchen Stil er aufweist- ist ein unabdingbares Element in den Feuchtzonen von Badezimmern.

DESIGN

DISEÑO

Options include eclectic, minimalist, oriental, classic, contemporary or avant-garde styles, but the most important factor of design is the feeling evoked. The bathroom is a personal space or, at the very least, a family one. Its exclusive nature means that its design will be defined by personal taste and comfort above all else.

Things like the bathroom's size, the type of furniture used, the decoration, the distribution of different facilities, usage, the type of materials, the range of colors and the design do not necessarily have to be in keeping with the overall style of the house, although it usually is in practice. It would be uncommon to find a classic style bedroom in a house created in the avant-garde style or vice-versa, although there are no set rules regarding such cases and the bathroom can include any variants the inhabitants may choose.

Ecléctico, minimalista, oriental, clásico, contemporáneo, de vanguardia, lo más importante de su diseño es la sensación que produce. El baño es una habitación personal o en todo caso familiar, a la que muy pocas personas que no pertenezcan a este núcleo tienen acceso. Por ello su concepto responde más a gustos personales y comodidad que a ninguna otra consideración.

Desde sus dimensiones, el tipo de muebles, la decoración, la distribución de los diferentes servicios, el uso, hasta el tipo de materiales y la paleta de colores, el diseño del cuarto de baño no necesariamente tiene que responder al estilo general de la casa, aunque lo más común es que así suceda. Difícilmente podrá verse una habitación de estilo muy clásico en una residencia de vanguardia y viceversa, aunque sobre ese particular no hay nada escrito y el baño puede tener todas las variantes que los moradores deseen.

Qu'il soit éclectique, minimaliste, oriental, classique, contemporain, avant-gardiste, l'important avec le design, c'est l'effet qu'il produit. La salle de bain est toujours une pièce personnelle et familiale où entrent peu de personnes étrangères au foyer. C'est pour cette raison que le design choisi répondra d'abord aux goûts des occupants tout en restant pratique.

Le design d'une salle de bain , en commençant par ses dimensions, son mobilier, sa décoration, ses séparations spécifiques, l'utilisation que l'on en fait et en terminant par le type de matériaux et la gamme de couleurs choisis, peut ne pas être identique au style qui prédomine dans le reste de la maison, bien que ce soit souvent le cas. Une salle de bain très classique dans une maison avant-gardiste (ou vice-versa) ne sera pas toujours d'un très bon goût. Toutefois il n'existe aucune règle écrite interdisant ces choix et les habitants d'un lieu ont tout le loisir d'opter pour la salle de bain la plus originale qui existe.

Ob eklektisch, minimalistisch, oriental, modern oder avantgardistisch, am wichtigsten am Design ist das Gefühl, das es hervorruft. Das Badezimmer ist ein persönlicher und sicherlich auch familiärer Ort, zu dem nur wenige Personen, die nicht zur Familie gehören, Zugang haben. Daher werden hier vor allem die persönlichen Geschmäcker und die Bequemlichkeit berücksichtigt.

Angefangen bei den Ausmassen, über den Möbeltyp, die Dekoration, die Aufteilung der unterschiedlichen Servicebereiche, den Gebrauch, bis hin zur Art der Materialien und der Farbpalette, muss das Design nicht unbedingt mit dem allgemeinen Stil des Hauses übereinstimmen, obwohl es meistens doch der Fall ist. Es ist schwer vorstellbar, dass das Badezimmer sehr klassisch eingerichtet ist und das restliche Haus einen avantgardistischen Stil aufweist oder umgekehrt. Obwohl es darüber nichts Schriftliches gibt und das Badezimmer alle Varianten haben kann, die die Hausbewohner wünschen.

The classic overtones of the mirror frame provide a pleasant contrast with the avant-garde design of the washbasins and the visual texture of the wall's wooden covering.

El marco del espejo, de reminiscencias clásicas, contrasta con el diseño vanguardista de los lavabos y la textura visual del recubrimiento de madera del muro.

Le cadre du miroir, de style classique, contraste avec le design avant-gardiste des lavabos et l'apparence du revêtement mural en bois.

Der Rahmen des Spiegels ist offensichtlich klassisch und kontrastiert mit dem avantgardistischen Design der Waschbecken und der visuellen Textur der Holzverkleidung an der Wand.

TIPS - ASTUCES - TIPPS
- *Deep basins will cut down on splashing.*
- *Optar por lavabos profundos te ayudará a evitar el salpicadero de agua.*
- *Choisir des lavabos profonds, c'est un moyen de ne pas éclabousser la pièce.*
- *Werden tiefe Waschbecken ausfgewählt, hilft dies dabei Spritzwasser zu vermeiden.*

The rich veins
of marble set
the tone for
the bathroom's
ambience.

L'élément primordial
qui donne une
atmosphère particulière
à cette salle de bain
est ici constitué par
le marbre aux veines
prononcées.

La veta de los
mármoles es el
punto de partida
para crear toda
la atmósfera del
baño.

Die Maserung des
Marmors ist der
Ausgangspunkt für
die Schaffung der
gesamten Atmosphäre
im Badezimmer.

TIPS - ASTUCES - TIPPS
• *If your bathroom boasts a lot of space, don't saturate it. Enjoy the benefits of spaciousness.*
• *Si el espacio de tu baño es amplio, no lo satures, goza de sus ventajas.*
• *Si votre salle de bain est de bonne taille, ne la surchargez pas et profitez de l'espace.*
• *Wenn das Badezimmer gross ist, sollte es nicht zu voll gestellt werden, vielmehr sind die Vorteile zu nutzen.*

TIPS - ASTUCES - TIPPS
- *Large marble slabs can be used to create compartments in a bathroom giving it a modern look and making it easy to clean.*
- *Utiliza grandes placas de mármol para crear compartimentos en un baño, lucirá moderno y será de fácil limpieza.*
- *Utilisez des grandes plaques de marbre pour créer des espaces différents et la salle de bain aura l'air plus moderne et sera plus facile à maintenir propre.*
- *Werden grosse Marmorplatten zum Abtrennen von Kabinen im Badezimmer verwendet, sieht dies modern aus und ist leicht zu reinigen.*

The feeling of freshness generated by the design comes from its total transparency and orderliness.

La transparencia absoluta y la nitidez del diseño transmiten una grata sensación de frescura en este cuarto de baño.

Associée ici à un design caractérisé par la clarté, une transparence complète donne à cette salle de bain une sensation de fraîcheur.

Die absolute Transparenz und Schärfe des Designs vermitteln den angenehmen Eindruck von Frische.

TIPS - ASTUCES - TIPPS
- A sense of symmetry can be achieved by repeating shapes.
- La repetición de formas conduce a lograr la sensación de simetría.
- Les mêmes formes déclinées plusieurs fois confèrent une certaine symétrie à l'ensemble.
- Die Wiederholung von Formen führt zu einem Eindruck von Symmetrie.

A minimalist design with the natural color and texture of onyx.

Un design minimaliste grâce à la texture et à la couleur naturelle de l'onyx.

Un diseño minimalista con la textura y el color natural del ónix.

Ein minimalistisches Design mit der natürlichen Textur und Farbe des Onyx.

TIPS - ASTUCES - TIPPS
- *Why not create an interplay of light and shade in your bathroom?*
- *Anímate a hacer de tu baño un juego de claroscuros.*
- *N'hésitez pas à jouer sur le clair-obscur dans votre salle de bain.*
- *Spiele in deinem Badezimmer mit hellen und dunklen Farben.*

Avant-garde furniture will provide a touch of originality for the bathroom, wherever it is located in the house.

Los muebles de estilo vanguardista dan un toque de originalidad al cuarto de baño, cualquiera que sea su estilo o ubicación dentro de la casa.

Les meubles de style avant-gardiste apportent de l'originalité dans cette salle de bain quel que soit son emplacement dans la maison.

Die Möbel im avantgardistischen Stil verleihen dem Badezimmer einen Touch Originalität, gleichgültig wo sich dieser Raum im Haus befindet.

TIPS - ASTUCES - TIPPS
- *Designer bathroom furniture must be highly practical and not restricted to a merely decorative role.*
- *Los muebles de diseño para baño deben ser particularmente prácticos y no quedarse en la estética.*
- *Les meubles design pour une salle de bain doivent d'abord être pratiques et pas simplement esthétiques.*
- *Designmöbel im Badezimmer müssen neben dem ästhtischen Aspekt vor allem auch praktisch sein.*

TIPS - ASTUCES - TIPPS
- An original bathtub will require space to stand out.
- Si seleccionas una tina original dale el espacio adecuado para que luzca.
- Si vous optez pour une baignoire originale, placez-la dans un espace suffisamment important pour la mettre en valeur.
- Bei Auswahl einer originellen Badewanne, sollte ihr auch genügend Platz zukommen, damit sie wirken kann.

The practical requirements of the bathroom have been comfortably resolved in a relatively small space with functional furniture.

Las funciones del cuarto de baño han sido resueltas cómodamente por sus muebles, en un espacio relativamente pequeño.

Les fonctions principales de la salle de bain ont été résolues astucieusement dans un espace relativement restreint, avec des meubles fonctionnels.

Die Funktionen des Badezimmers wurden in einem relativ kleinen Raum bequem gelöst, indem funktionelle Möbel verwendet wurden.

The main attraction of a modern bathroom can sometimes be its sheer stylishness.

La decoración, muchas veces de gran clase y distinción, puede ser el principal punto de atracción de un cuarto de baño moderno.

La décoration, très souvent raffinée et de grande classe, peut être l'élément-clé pour une salle de bain esthétique et moderne.

Die Dekoration ist oft von grosser Klasse und kann der hauptsächliche Attraktionspunkt in einem modernen Badezimmer sein.

TIPS - ASTUCES - TIPPS
- Originality is a very appealing feature in any design, including the bathroom.
- En cualquier diseño, aún en el baño, la originalidad es altamente atractiva.
- L'originalité d'un design, quel qu'il soit et y compris pour une salle bain, sera toujours un atout majeur.
- Bei jedem Design und sogar auch im Badezimmer, ist die Originalität besonders attratkiv.

LIGHT

LUZ

LUMIÈRE

LICHT

The bathroom has been created with plenty of light in view of its nature and role, but other resources can also be harnessed to further enhance its illumination or regulate and tone the light inside it. Some bathrooms use brightly colored materials with a very subtle visual impact to achieve this, while others rely more on darker, stronger tones to grab our attention with the light providing an elegant setting full of character. A more distinguished ambience can be generated through the use of formal tones, such as black and gray. Another option is to create contrasts between different tones to regulate and define the type of light required.

In each case, the solution will depend on the personal tastes of the home's inhabitants. The materials use to build it, decorate it and for furniture will determine just how much light there is in the bathroom. The brighter they are, the more light will be generated, and the opposite will also apply.

Por naturaleza, el cuarto de baño ha sido creado con la intención de ser un espacio lleno de luz; pero hay otros que requieren la aplicación de ciertos recursos para parecer más luminosos o para regular y matizar la luminosidad que priva en la habitación. Algunos utilizan materiales claros, visualmente muy ligeros; otros, por el contrario buscan los tonos oscuros y fuertes que atraen nuestra atención y la luz que generan crean un ambiente elegante y con personalidad. Los tonos más formales, como el negro y los grises crean un ambiente distinguido. Otros más recurren al contraste entre diferentes tonalidades para regular el tipo de luz que desean en su habitación.

En todo caso, la solución depende del gusto de quienes vayan a utilizarlo. Los materiales empleados en la construcción, en la decoración o en el mobiliario son reflejantes de la mayor o menor luminosidad que se pretenda dar al baño. A más claridad mayor luminosidad y viceversa.

De par sa fonction, la salle de bain a été créée pour être une pièce très illuminée. On a toutefois besoin pour certaines salles de bain d'avoir recours à des procédés particuliers pour les éclairer ou pour réguler et tamiser la lumière qui domine trop la pièce. Pour y parvenir, on peut utiliser des matériaux clairs et très légers visuellement parlant. À l'inverse, on peut rechercher des couleurs sombres et foncées que l'on remarque d'emblée et la lumière qui en résulte transformera la pièce en un endroit élégant et personnalisé. Les couleurs plus austères, comme le noir et les différents gris, donneront naissance à une salle de bain raffinée. On peut aussi opter pour un contraste entre plusieurs couleurs afin de réguler une lumière particulière pour qu'elle convienne à la pièce.

Dans tous les cas, la solution adoptée dépendra des goûts de ceux qui vont utiliser cette pièce. Les matériaux employés pour sa construction, sa décoration ou son mobilier seront pensés pour répondre à l'éclairage désiré. Plus la salle de bain sera claire, mieux elle sera illuminée. L'inverse est aussi exact.

Aufgrund seiner Natur ist das Badezimmer ein Ort, an dem viel Licht vorhanden sein soll; ist dies nicht der Fall, so sind bestimmte Mittel notwendig, um mehr Licht zu schaffen oder das Licht zu regulieren bzw. abzutönen. Dazu verwenden einige helle Materialien, die visuell sehr leicht sind; andere benutzen hingegen dunkle und starke Farben, die unsere Aufmerksamkeit auf sich ziehen und eine elegante Atmosphäre schaffen. Andere wiederum greifen auf den Kontrast zwischen verschiedenen Farbtönen zurück, um die Lichtart zu regulieren, die sie in dem Raum beabsichtigen.

In jedem Fall hängt die Lösung von den Vorlieben der Benutzer ab. Die beim Bau, der Dekoration oder den Möbeln verwendeten Materialien spiegeln wider, ob die Helligkeit im Bad gross oder eher gering sein soll. Werden helle Farben verwendet, führt dies zu mehr Helligkeit und umgekehrt.

A large, very
brightly lit
bathroom includes
space for a
changing area
and storage
furniture, but not
at the expense
of the bathroom's
practical role.

Une pièce de
grandes dimensions,
généreusement
éclairée, où l'on trouve
un endroit pour les
dressings et les meubles
de rangement sans
pour autant réduire
l'espace réservé à la
salle de bain.

Una habitación
de grandes
dimensiones,
profusamente
iluminada, reserva
un lugar para
los vestidores
y muebles de
guardado.

Ein Raum mit
grossen Ausmassen
und grosszügigem
Lichteinfall bietet Platz
für die Ankleidebereiche
und Möbel zum
Aufbewahren, ohne
dass dabei die
eigentlichen Funktionen
des Bades beeinträchtigt
werden.

TIPS - ASTUCES - TIPPS
- *A vital factor in any boudoir is the quality of both daylight and artificial light.*
- *La calidad de la luz, natural y artificial, es un componente esencial en un tocador.*
- *La qualité de la lumière, naturelle ou artificielle, est un élément essentiel pour un cabinet de toilette.*
- *Die Qualität von natürlichem und künstlichem Licht ist ein wesentlicher Faktor im Bad.*

Light from the
outside can be
regulated or
directed at specific
points by using
skylights and
soffits.

La luz proveniente
del exterior puede
regularse o
dirigirse aciertos
puntos mediante el
uso de plafones y
tragaluces.

La lumière, qui
vient de l'extérieur,
peut être réglée
et orientée vers
certains endroits
grâce aux faux-
plafonds et
aux ouvertures
que l'on y a
pratiquées.

Das Licht, das aus
dem Äusseren
hereinscheint
kann reguliert
oder gerichtet
werden, indem
Plafonds oder
Luken verwendet
werden.

TIPS · ASTUCES · TIPPS
• Lighting can be used to create some wonderful effects that we will enjoy every time we use the bathroom.
• A través de la iluminación se consiguen efectos insuperables que podemos disfrutar diariamente.
• Une illumination adéquate produit des effets sans comparaison que l'on peut apprécier tous les jours.
• Mit Hilfe der Beleuchtung entstehen unübertreffliche Effekte, an denen wir uns jeden Tag erfreuen können.

Artificial light always plays a vital role in setting the ambience of a room thanks to the maneuverability and quality of the light projected.

La iluminación artificial siempre desempeña un papel sobresaliente en el diseño de la atmósfera una habitación por la ductilidad y la calidad de la luz que proyecta.

L'éclairage artificiel, grâce aux variations possibles et á la qualité de sa lumiére, joue toujours un rôle prépondérant pour donner une certaine atmosphère à une pièce.

Das künstliche Licht spielt immer eine besondere Rolle in Bezug auf das Design der Atmosphäre eines Raumes, und dies aufgrund seiner Dehnbarkeit und der Lichtqualität.

TIPS - ASTUCES - TIPPS
- *Reflective surfaces can be placed opposite each to other generate a superb sparkling effect.*
- *Si colocas superficies reflejantes frente a frente, los destellos que generen con la luz serán grandiosos.*
- *Placer des surfaces réfléchissantes les unes face aux autres génère de superbes éclats lumineux.*
- *Werden spiegelnde Oberflächen gegenübergestellt, verursacht das Licht ein grandioses Glitzern.*

TIPS - ASTUCES - TIPPS

• The use of lighting directed downwards to skim across the surfaces of the bathroom will create a welcoming ambience.

• Conviene para un ambiente acogedor iluminar con luces descendentes y rasantes.

• Un éclairage plongeant et rasant est tout indiqué pour une pièce que l'on souhaite agréable.

• Zum Erzielen einer gemütlichen Atmosphäre, sind absteigende und rasante Lichter geeignet.

Los domos y
la iluminación
indirecta matizan
suavemente
la textura de
los muros y la
intensidad de la
luz.

Skylights and
indirect lighting
tone the texture
of the walls and
the intensity of the
light.

Les toits en verre et
l'éclairage indirect
modifient avec
douceur l'aspect
des murs et la
lumière dans la
pièce.

Die Öffnungen
in der Decke
und die indirekte
Beleuchtung tönen
weich die Textur der
Wände und die
Lichtintensität ab.

El sitio reservado para la ducha se enriquece estéticamente con la veta del mármol.

Marble veins bring out the visual splendor of the shower area.

Le marbre veiné esthétise l'endroit réservé pour la douche.

Der Bereich, der für die Dusche reserviert ist, wird ästhetisch durch die Maserung des Marmors bereichert.

TIPS - ASTUCES - TIPPS
- A well-designed shower unit can become the best window in the house.
- Bien resuelta, la regadera puede ser la mejor vitrina de una casa.
- Bien pensée, la douche peut être la meilleure vitrine de la maison.
- Bei Anwendung einer guten Lösung, kann die Dusche wie die schönste Vitrine des Hauses aussehen.

TIPS · ASTUCES · TIPPS

- *Lighting projected from concealed sources will afford a pleasant sense of mystique to the room.*
- *Las fuentes de luz que ocultan su procedencia generan un agradable misterio.*
- *Les sources d'éclairage dissimulées donnent un certain mystère à la pièce.*
- *Die Lichtquellen, deren Herkunft nicht sichtbar ist, führen zu einem angenehmen Mysterium.*

A feeling of elegance and stylishness is created by light from the lamps.

El diseño y la luz proveniente de las lámparas provocan una grata sensación de elegancia y distinción al cuarto de baño.

Le design et la lumière des lampes transforment agréablement la pièce pour en faire un lieu élégant et raffiné.

Das Design und das Licht, das aus den Leuchten stammt, verursachen einen angenehmen Eindruck von Eleganz und Vornehmheit.

La luz se filtra por un gran ventanal y resalta la calidad de los materiales empleados en muros y muebles.

Light is filtered through a large window to highlight the intrinsic qualities of the materials of the walls and furniture.

La lumière, filtrée par une grande fenêtre translucide, fait ressortir les qualités des matériaux employés pour les murs et les meubles.

Das Licht dringt durch das grosse Fenster ein und hebt die Qualität der für die Wände und Möbel verwendeten Materialien hervor.

TIPS · ASTUCES · TIPPS
- *Highly polished surfaces will shine in unexpected ways.*
- *Superficies muy pulidas garantizan destellos de luz sorpresivos.*
- *Des surfaces très bien polies produisent assurément de surprenants éclats lumineux.*
- *Hochpolierte Oberflächen garantieren überraschende Lichtreflexe.*

architectonic   arquitectónicos   architectoniques   architektonische

photographic   fotográficos   photographiques   fotografische

Printed in January 2009 in China. Published by AM
Editores S.A. de C.V.
Se terminó de imprimir el mes de enero del 2009
en China. El cuidado de la edición estuvo a cargo
de AM Editores S.A. de C.V.